youthwriterscamp.com

Greetings to All!

Welcome to those who have decided to give this young author's first book a read. We believe in youth and their stories so much that we believe we can be a part of helping them tell their stories. We have been so inspired to see them grow and change.

Our Youth Writers Camp provides continuous opportunities for healthy emotional expression within a safe and supportive community. Our goal is to both to help young people cope through writing and to motivate them to develop their own streams of revenue.

Brandon C Allen, LLC is actively engaging today's youth with an aim to increase mental and emotional health outcomes. However, we understand that our efforts to positively impact the mental and emotional health of this current generation won't reach maximum effectiveness unless we have the support of the entire community.

THIS IS WHERE YOU COME IN.

Through the things they discovered about themselves, the lessons about mental health, and the coping techniques they garnered during this time, it is our job as a community to continue to cultivate their development and empower them to shift their own realities into the best versions designed for them. Our hope is that these students feel loved, cared for, and equipped enough to continue to heal and process with healthy coping tools and creative avenues. Thank you for investing in this student, one poem at a time.

Students, congratulations and I am proud of all you accomplished. Continue to be all you are meant to be.

Brandon Allen, Author and Founder of Youth Writers Camp

Dear Kameron,

Do you know what you just did? Seriously. Think about it. You wrote your first book. Did you know that a recent survey of 2,000 U.S. respondents reveals just 15 percent have started writing a book, and a mere six percent have gotten halfway through?

You beat the odds. Many say what they are going to do. Some start it, then abandon it—very few finish. You finished.

Growing up, I always kept a journal. Writing and playing the piano were my first loves. Had I known of a program like this and had a teacher like Brandon Allen, I would have been an author at seven years old. Serving alongside Brandon and making many young authors' dreams come true is a blessing.

Remember, this is just your first step in a long and adventurous journey. Always write. Writing can serve as a constant and reliable best friend.

With love and poetry,

Camari Carter Hawkins
Author and Founder of Mama's Kitchen Press

LEARNING TO CONTROL IT

KAMERON GARNETT

MAMA'S
KITCHEN
PRESS

Learning to Control It
©2023 Kameron Garnett
ISBN: 979-8-9893829-0-3

First Edition, 2023

Printed in the United States of America

Cover Concept by Kameron Garnett
Cover & Layout Design by Emily Anne Evans

*This book is dedicated to my mom
and my family for supporting me
every step of the way.*

CONTENTS

FOREWORD

Kameron is my son, my love, my everything. All I have ever wanted for him is great things. My mission has been to show him how to achieve it for himself. I'm so proud of Kameron for sharing his thoughts and emotions with the world in *Learning to Control It*. He is so strong and powerful — I truly believe he can do anything he wants in the world.

Kameron: Keep searching and don't stop reaching, baby. I'll love you always.

Kiran Nieves Álvarez

LEARNING TO CONTROL IT

UNTOLD WRATH

I was angry with my friend;
I told my wrath, my wrath did end.
I was angry with my foe;
I told it not, my wrath did grow.
And I watered it in fears,
Night and morning with my tears.
And I survived it with smiles,
And with soft crying mornings,
And it grew both day and night
Till it bore an apple bright.
And my foe saw it shine,
And he knew that it was mine.
And into my garden stole,
When the night had, I unveiled it to my foe.
In the morning glad I see,
My foe was now a friend to me.

CONTROLLED

The sheet shielding my anger is ripping at the seams
A burst of sound erupts from me as angry thoughts invade
I want to stop but the words keep flowing
I can't form a sentence
All I may form is rage
The anger buried deep inside has been let outside of its cage
My facade is failing as a tear falls from my cheek
The taunts and jokes about me have finally made me weak
I ask to go to the bathroom to flush my feelings
A waterfall emerges from my eyes
I scream in silence as the sink catches my tears
Paper towels wipe the residue
I realize through the drops
I am just a guy
People will disagree with me and the insults will last
And when I comprehend that
I return to class

STUCK INSIDE

During the pandemic,
I felt fine, I was innocent
I didn't know what was happening
A week of school: Amazing!
Another week and then another
A month, now two
I saw the deaths, the families broken
I had just moved, so I adjusted quickly
My family got sick
Leading to me being sick
I was now infected with a virus called COVID
The deaths started slowing as the world kept rolling
Eventually it ended

THANK YOU

I used to be mad
I learned to be happy
You led me to the land of happiness
I wasn't here, you put me on
Now that I'm here, you went and gone
You were there for me when even I wasn't
You saw past my smile
You understood
You were nice about it
When I was shy, you had pride
You inspired me to see the world in a different light
Even if you had sleepless nights,
You always made me feel alright
You spoke about it,
I poked around it
Now I'm not embarrassed to talk about my feelings
Thank you my friend, you were there until the end

I'M NOT AFRAID

Endless nights awake
Bears, you beasts beware
For now I'm not afraid,
For now I am aware
I see you monstrous creatures,
You don't even try to hide
You don't know that when I unleash my rage,
All of you will die
But I won't; I must change
I must change for the better
I'm stuck in the past
I'm still sending letters; I must become better
My mind is one of the best, but I can be less
I don't have to be great
I'm not a mistake
My confidence is too high, I don't mean to boast
But now I'm better, so let's have a toast

WITHHELD TEMPER

Hold your temper for self sake.
This is the prudent way:
Often when it is not controlled,
It hands the body down to the clay.

When anger takes our feeble mind and weak heart
And conscience asks the mind to obey,
We find our self left for dead
And our sins have gone to play.

Temper governed and tongues held back
Keeps peace day by day.
When the body discharges the violence of temper,
Friendship tears away.

Eternity is for ever and ever,
Life is only a short stay,
For it will all end soon,
You will be led astray.

I'M SO MAD

I'm so mad I could scream

I'm so mad I could spit

Turn over a table

Run off in a spring

I'm so mad I could yell

I could tear out my hair

Throw a rock through a window

Or wrestle a bear!

On thinking it over

I will not leave home

But I'll put all my anger

Right here in this poem

I'm feeling much better

Like peaches and cream

For a poem is the best way

Of letting off steam

MY ANGER

Anger is a thing that brings

Negative and sad things

Find a way to control your feeling

Don't let them catch you kneeling

Anger is an emotion

That can be compared to an explosion

But it doesn't have to be that way

You can't control it or keep it at bay

Anger can hurt and it can harm

When you feel it, it is reason for alarm

Go for a walk, just cool off

It controls you when you walk and talk

When you don't give in to it

When you don't throw a fit

You will find control you will have

And for that, you'll be glad.

BROKEN HEART

It is not so much what you say

As the manner in which you say it

It is not so much the language you use

As the tones in which you convey it

The words may be mild and fair

And the tones may pierce like a dart

The words may be soft as the summer air

And the tones may break the heart

For words come from the mind

And grow by study and art

But the tones leap forth from the inner self

And reveal the state of the heart

I AM AFRAID

I am afraid
Death does not sleep
I am afraid
But I won't be a sheep
I am afraid
I will escape
I am afraid
Courage I will shape
I'm going to be great
I won't be shy
I will shape myself into a great guy
I can do this
I can survive
The will to power through
Resides deep inside
...And I found it

ABOUT THE AUTHOR

Kameron is a 12-year-old gamer turned author. He still loves games though. He lives in Kissimmee, Florida with his little sister, dad, mom, and brother. He couldn't have written this book without his brother, the inspiration behind many poems. Here's a little game: figure out which ones he inspired.